Wherever I Go, There You Are

fay marie mcdonald

PARTRIDGE
A Penguin Random House Company

To order additional copies of this book, contact
Toll Free 800 101 2657 (Singapore)
Toll Free 1 800 81 7340 (Malaysia)
orders.singapore@partridgepublishing.com

www.partridgepublishing.com/singapore

Where Ever I Go, There You Are, is the companion to Grief is a River. This book is a graphic description of the workings of the human heart, and universal dilemmas. A search to unravel the ties that bind us. The past has ways of leaving an indelible impression that we are not always aware of ~until we are.~ Misunderstandings in the daily humanity of living can be forgiven, can be repaired, and with an open heart I share my sense of the solemn beauty of prose and poetry, in spite of, or because of, the inadequacies of love.

A work of art that retraces the conquest of happiness would be a revolutionary one.

Noces, Albert Camus {1937}

2014

Age is a funny thing.

There is my actual birth date. And there have been many things I'd wished had never happened.

Unclaimable.

Regrets irretrievable.

Has anyone lived without regrets?

I think not.

I have done heaps of things, some challenging, others interesting, given all I was capable of giving, often wishing I'd had more knowing in an off-beat kind of way.

But I hadn't.

I have given life my best shot.

It is time to be more truthful with myself, more understanding of me. I'd thought I had been.

Be clearer, find my voice in the threads of me, be even more aware of others in the right way and be as kind as I can. Many things are making more sense to me than they ever have.

Kindness had lifted its head from the crowd.

If I had a motto to live by, which I don't . . . by trial and error I would be as kind as I could be, to all and sundry whoever they may be.

I don't have to love everyone. At least I can be kind.

1

If I haven't made mistakes, I haven't lived.

Before dropping off the mortal coil I want to leave no gaps.

Wisdom could be mine if I no longer measured myself against anyone.

And my curiosity of other people's stories, all kinds of fictions, plays, movies, even at times the seamier sides of lives. The whole box and dice of being human.

Is the balance between the good and the not so good such an unheralded discovery?

Others may wonder why I constantly read about the *grief* of others, yet it is their stories that have helped me understand more fully my own *grief*.

In reading "Relearning the World" the title of an article by Brooke Davis, who wrote the book Lost and Found, I read about her *grief* as "relearning the world of (her) experience.

Brooke Davis writes of moving back and forth and up and down and over and sideways through different stages of *grief* for as long as she is there. Brooke Davis became aware that grief is simply a part of everything she does.

Everything she says.

Everything she writes.

Everything she is.

For me too, *grief* didn't just go somewhere else.

It is a part of who I for all time will be.

Friends and families may show us who they are, with how they act, depending on what's happening in their lives. They aren't always able to give us a true picture.

It can be confusing.

Here am I thinking of music, of plays, the books I love that I would almost die for. These are some of the things that have helped me to live in ways I couldn't have comprehended if I hadn't read, or had the experience of them.

I have become more insatiably eager for experiences no matter how they arrive on my doorstep.

When I was very young I learnt about life from my grandmother, simple everyday things about how to be and how to love.

And from my mother and my father.

My grandmother became a widow before I was born.

My grandfather dying within a few short days of being struck down with tetanus in his forties A tiny splinter in his finger had left my grandmother with ten children and little income.

Her youngest only two years of age.

She had experienced grief at the same age as I had, in my forties.

Had my grandmother after weeks and months of grieving been able to let go of any understanding she may once have had? How had she found a way beyond grief?

Grief

is my companion
fate declares time allocates
I lived   on and beyond
in a time of   abeyance
suspended   almost dormant
*   then reality hit.*
With grief as my companion
I set sail on
that spindly barely
known highway.

2014

My grandmother wasn't only warm-hearted, she carried a natural air of pure compassion in everything she did.

And with her I had great fun doing . . . whatever!!

No misunderstandings.

We did anything we wanted to do. Living with her when my mother had so often been rushed away to hospital. Understanding years later that that was why I never did have the brother or sister I had often been promised.

With her I didn't go to school if I didn't want to.

We had had magical times together doing the simplest of things.

Were those times as magical for her?

It had seemed so.

Remembering my grandmother saying before I was sent away to boarding school at eight years of age:

Be kind to people no matter what, and they will be kind to you.

My grandmother gave me gifts to last
courage she said was the answer to life
her gaze held strength, joy and love.
I speak to her still when my courage wanes.
Pain is gain in courage contained.
(12ᵗʰ August 1989)

5

My Grandmother

2014

The day is hot. The air is warm. I look onto our garden filled with the unruly explosion of spring.

Azaleas as big as fists.

I stare into green centered white flowers thinking . . .

You're not young anymore.

You can't believe just how quickly not being young happened.

Held today in an aura of disclosure, hinting at something out there in the open blue of the sky.

I am present. I am a folk ballad tangled in with elusive questions yielding images . . .

Me as a young child alone on a beach at four years of age.

Purple-spotted pyjamas clinging to my legs.

I must have had a scared, lost look on my face the day I ran away.

Running down the side pathway to climb the front fence.

Couldn't I have walked through the open gate?

But I had climbed the fence for some wacky reason. Did I have to make it more difficult for myself before running away, heading for the clear blue bay?

Why at four years of age had I a need to run away?

Certainly not from my young teen-aged parents.

I just had to.

Vaguely aware of being on the beach, my mother finding me there, holding me, then furiously shaking me before clasping me, holding me close saying "You must never ever run away again. Promise me."

And the tears.

Arms tight around me.

My mother, a winged chariot taking me back to a safe place.

My home.

Oh! The comfort of it!

Give Meaning
　　Sense time.
　　　　Let go all that is irreparable.
　　　　　　Gather honey explore constantly and dance.

2014

The moon, almost translucent, shines through the sky-light in our bedroom.

Offering me what?

Feel the moonlight, sink into joy, choose memories in holding the delicate balance of his presence.

Out of bed at last I wander through our rambling garden. The feeling of Glenn is in the garden with me as a whiff of mint wafts up from beneath my feet.

I twist a sprig of rosemary between my fingers.

Pungent, woody and new.

Mornings for me had once been a time when tiny animals, frogs, all living creatures could hold me to ransom . . . but all I could do back then was climb back into bed.

Bury myself under the covers.

Life changed in an instant

The tender gravity of it awakened me to sorrow . . . I held it.

Kindness sent me out to buy bread and milk . . . I held that too.

I bought bacon and eggs and greens . . . I held them all.

I tied shoelaces . . . I went through the motions . . . a robot.

On the longest of days sorrow was to become my friend.

loss softened. . . . I breathed in the air.

I trembled . . . I trembled into grey.

Gifts

in a whim of yearning
skinned with regrets
exposed wounds found strengths

the smallest of things sought the clearest

I talked to myself
I said I was sorry
for what?

In gifts of yearning
I found my way.

Viewing the U T S Gehry Building for the first time.

2014

Yesterday, the past, the present, and the future were mingled together as I stepped out of Kristian's car. My first sighting of the almost complete iconic Gehry building at U T S in Sydney.

Kristian, my grandson, a young architect has been involved since its inception.

Surprised to hear myself saying . . .

"The feeling this building gives me, Kristian, is more than me or you, it's more than us."

He'd smiled, probably wondering what the hell I was talking about.

A serendipitous moment.

The brickwork of the structure set in undulating extraordinary patterns, the continuous flowing movements flanked by walls of glass. From where Kristian and I were standing the workers looked like a myriad of ant-like people clambering helter-skelter all over the site.

Is it foolish to think this waving, weaving, structure of bricks, of people, and of a particular place in time, could stop my heart from rusting?

I recall a quotation by the architect describing the skin of his Bilbao Museum as:

"the randomness of curves designed to catch light."

I once lost light.

The side seams of our lives had all but been ripped apart.

There was a time before day left and night came, when a sadness would linger in that space between evening coming and day leaving.

Waiting, always waiting.

Is great sorrow simply to be accepted as an absolute?

For me it took a long time to come to that way of thinking.

Kristian talking with Frank Gehry on the Opening Day.

Let it Happen

A bird chirps at your window.
He sings to you.

In the shadowy rainforest
leaves rock themselves awake.

What needs remembering?
What needs to be forgotten?

The sun comes out.
Let it happen.

2014

No longer am I struck by grief.

I embraced grief as if it were knitting me more closely to the person Glenn would have wanted me to become.

In the way happenings had linked me to things I hadn't known could be there.

Within me or for me.

Years ago when my children were growing up I hadn't had a reason to change anything.

I wasn't drowning.

My life wasn't a disaster.

We had had great times together by the river, that beautiful river. Our home the setting off point where our children's friends so often had set sail every weekend.

Thinking of the tiny silver cup handed around each week to the winner of the sailing race.

My thoughts today are of how back then I had become aware of changes happening, unrecognised wonderings that I couldn't at first understand.

My everyday living had had an "edge" to it that hadn't been obvious. Life became splintered and I began to understand why.

I had a need to find the right words, at the right time, about what our life had become.

I found the right words.

Once out of the box they could not be put back.

Everything in our world shifted. A sad day for everyone.

I made choices, not always right, but right or wrong they were completely mine.

The years on the river came to an end.

Is there ever a right time for a family to fall apart?

2014

Families fall apart every day.

There are many things that can be saved. If you have a mind to save them.

Though what once was could never be again.

Happy times not forgotten.

I chose to build on what I then had.

Life was ours to be lived . . . I remember1973, yet here am I in the year 2014. held In a sea of memories, and misplacing my space in time.

I'm standing on the corner of a street in Rome, wind blowing around me, papers scattering, people rushing.

Glenn, Fiona and Julie, grown children running towards me, laughing at their first taste of Europe, and loving it.

Glenn the leader of the pack.

All five of us, a complete family, discovering Italians to be so engaging, inviting disarray, expressing their passion for life in the ordinary everydayness of living it.

Blown away by their open, kindly understanding of how delighted we all were to be a part of their world.

Picturing all five of us, laughing, climbing into the smallest car we had ever seen.

A Baby Fiat.

All squashed together. Peas in a pod. Driving, driving, in and out of the crazy traffic in Rome. This friendly bald-headed Italian drove us everywhere, with the crinkly smile of a good man. We hadn't even shared a language, he so excited to be showing us his city.

As if we for the first time had presented Rome to him through our eyes.

Him pointing, smiling at us, and with us, laughing, continually calling . . .

Roman wall. Roman wall. Roman wall.

Moon dreams on a tightrope
Possibilities in the texture of my day.
Intoxicating.
The light of day teasing a world, tranquil as
the curve of an egg's surface.
Moon dreams leave me wondering. . .
What happens to butterflies in winter?

My print of The Third Creek

An unusual connection. A landscape of our home and a slither of the bathroom.
We are surrounded by the rainforest, and by rock walls.
Rocks, rocks and more rocks

I stood on the Margins
I laughed softly.
Can anyone hear me?
Can I be . . . the Hero of my life?

2014

Has Frank Gehry, this trail-blazing architect, scrambled my thinking of Glenn my son?

Through shared memories Kristian had always had a clear picture of his uncle. Glenn's way of being as a twenty-three year old had been quietly different from many of his friends.

As a small child Glenn had been both tender and vulnerable.

At six years of age early one morning he'd released a tiny trapped mouse while everyone was sleeping in our shack by the river, I found him distraught standing in the kitchen beside the pot belly stove.

That day the river was turbulent, rain bucketing down in a storm's sweet release, him sobbing holding the empty mouse trap as if his world had come to an end, saying, "I had to let him free. I just had to."

As if his heart were breaking.

Protect what is precious.

We all share the same sky in the buzzing incompleteness of living.

Kristian, Caroline and the stairs.

2014

Years ago I had been inspired on reading an article about the Frank Gehry Museum in Bilbao.

Back then Kristian my grandson was barely a boy.

Clive Tompkins wrote:

"The greatest building of our time, a fantastic dream ship of undulating form in a cloak of titanium."

I have a surprising attachment to this unconventional, outlandish structure in our city created and designed by Gehry, the self-same architect. Now becoming a part of my everyday musings, thinking and writing.

I have no idea why.

Apart from Kristian's involvement as . . . and my interest in all that has been happening on the building over the last few years. This structure has seemed to have become, in a strange way, just a part of who I now am becoming. As if I am more alive, in a different way, as the U T S structure grows.

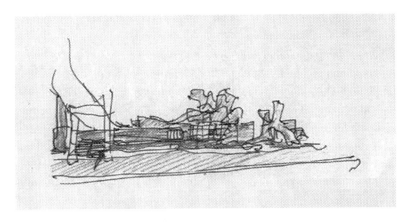

As Barbara Isenberg shows me in her book Conversations with Frank Gehry, a sketch like this is how the Museum in Bilbao came into fruition. It seems to be the beginnings of all of his buildings.

Gehry talks of the first Gehry building in Sydney, Australia, as first being sketched as a tree house with limbs reaching out in many directions.

His close friendship with many artists and their work seems, to have made an impression on the buildings he continues to design and build. Exciting that we in Australia are about to have a Gehry structure of our own.

2014

In the book *Conversations with Frank,* by Barbara Isenberg, Gehry talked of his life and his work. His answer to the questions about his grandmother was:

"I wish she was still here so I could tell her how important she was to me."

Gehry's grandmother was a kind of community Shaman. A healer. He would go with her to sick people's houses, and they would all sit and do vigil until they got better. Remembering going to one house where they applied suction cups to a man's back, then his grandmother took out a quill pen and started writing on his arm.

Gehry hadn't believed in any of it, but he'd loved his grandmother.

He was fascinated.

He lived with the images of him playing on the floor with her when he was a small child, to make tiny structures out of wooden blocks.

Saying to Barbara Isenberg that his grandparents were a haven from his parents who were a bit edgy.

Maybe that edginess is also a part of him creating these controversial buildings of unusual shapes and patterns. Reflected yesterday in walls of glass that in the U T S building appeared to be almost liquefied.

A captivating, soaring capricious space.

I imagine a kite flies aloft.

Almost mystical . . . whimsical . . . sorrow lets go the detail.

2010

Kristian returned from Los Angeles a few years ago.

Having spent three months being a part of Frank Gehry's team in the early stages of the building's creation.

Kristian returned with a book for me called Conversations with Frank Gehry by Barbara Isenberg.

On the fly leaf he wrote:

Dear Omi

I give you this book about a man.

He had a grandmother who was very influential in his life.

You have been very influential to mine.

I have many stories to tell.

Love you always

Kristian

Be Still

Place your cheek upon the soft earth.
listen.

Not to endless conversations of
grasses or shallow roots.

Not to beetles or the good worms.
Reach beyond time.

All too soon you
will not have a voice.

Wherever I Go, There You Are

2014

Between birth, and my acceptance of life, can I ever fully know what life is about?

If I listen closely maybe I will begin to understand.

The first time Kristian had taken me to view the still incomplete Gehry building in an inner city laneway I had stood there beside him wishing Glenn too was there beside us.

Poised in a gentle stillness, as if sound waves were swimming, circling us.

With a quiver of recognition . . . a quirky delight had lingered, holding the memory of the most important dream I had ever had . . .

A dream that was to become an installation in the rainforest beside the University in my final year.

Becoming my celebration of Glenn's short life.

Had I been just the observer of the dream?

Or was I an important part of being witness to re-creating what that dream had meant to me?

Had the dream given me the key to what I had had no choice but to do?

Find a way to live the way Glenn would have wanted each of us to live.

Myself, his father, Fiona, Julie and Kristian.

Trust memory.
Dreams your lynch pin under the squeak of stars.
What was not there until you made it?
Constrained in wisps of the yet to be consoled.
The significance of your life is too particular to be placed in
*   a box by*
any other but you.

2014

Photographs of a night, a time filled with memories and sighs.
Hard sweet wisdom carries its own pain for everyone.
Words for me can create a sense of a rhythm in my lived life in the
words I chose to place on the page.

Writing soothes me, it is my tranquilliser, my way to understand
me, and the actions of others.
An awareness of me If only for myself.

2014

When Gehry won the contract for the building in Spain, the question asked of him was:

"Can you create a building for Bilbao as great as the Sydney Opera House?"

His reply. "I will do my best."

"But I can't guarantee anything like that."

"That is a big ask."

He didn't adhere to our Opera House but he did present Bilboa with the Guggenheim Museum. These days praised by many, built on the shores of the Nervion River running into the Cantabrian Sea

The people of Bilbao were given their just rewards.

Both the Opera House and the Guggenheim Museum Bilboa are two of the most iconic buildings of the 20th century.

Possibly this building is to become a part of the commercial learning of our city, and though that kind of structure will never be as grand as an Opera House or a Museum, this building will no doubt create its own place in time.

Until the U T S Gehry building eventually comes to completion I will just have to wait and see.

2014

With Gehry was it like wafting in a breeze? Being taken, wherever?

But Gehry is questioning, controversial and extremely self-reliant.

He must have had a fearless audacity for difference in doing whatever he chooses to do, yet his respect for others was always there.

Am I a mystery of my own making, or just stitched together fragments?

A scramble of uniquely arranged experiences?

Are Gehry's flights of fancy, apparent in the U T S building here in my city, justifiable, when so many people are homeless?

We enter buildings every day in one way or another. The most fortunate of us even live in them.

Yet architecture on any scale can be art or it can be a disaster.

The more I read about Gehry, the more I am faced with a portrait of a simple, yet complex, man, both engaging and perceptive.

Understanding why his Museum in Bilbao, in its particular space, gave that city a feeling of lightness for all the world to admire.

Though never casting my eyes upon the actual Museum, just to picture the shape of it makes me smile.

The heart knows no distance.

Yet something relevant to me appears to be shifting as this structure Kristian has become a part of finds the way to be.

I once dived into the ocean at Seven Mile Beach before walking along that beach for hours.

I write about walking along the beach in my first book Grief is a River.

This photograph is a very different walk along Seven Mile Beach. Kristian gave me the photograph. Caroline had taken of us, footprints trailing behind in the sand. The photograph and the words a gift from Kristian to celebrate Mother's Day a couple of years ago.

A beach forever to hold special memories for me.

DEAR OMI,

THANK YOU FOR ALL OF YOUR
HELP WELL SINCE THE BEGIN
BUT ESPECIALLY FOR THE
PAST COUPLE OF YEARS.
NOW HERE'S LOOKING TO A
BRIGHT AND ENJOYABLE
FUTURE!

HAPPY MOTHERS DAY!

LOVE,
    KRISTIAN.

There is

a significance to our life

too particular

to be placed in a box

of anyone else's

making?

2014

In Bilbao Gehry had imagined billowing sails in a maritime setting. Steel resonated to the industrial history of the Basque country. On winning the contract for the "Bilbao Museum," Gehry's first response was: "It could be the chosen site, adapting the building to offices or a hotel. But not to a Museum."

A deadly silence had followed this comment.

"Bilbao" he later told them, "is a dirty messy industrial city. It has a forgiveness. I like industrial cities."

Later, much later, he suggested the right spot. Where the Museum now stands.

Bilbao, a steel city, needed metal.

Titanium caught his eye because Bilbao had lots of rain and lots of grey skies.

He found titanium to be buttery. He took a piece of titanium, nailed it onto a telephone post outside his office. He watched to see what it did in the light.

Boat imagery also often appeared in Gehry's structures, as it has in my life.

There was a special magic to living by a river. the Georges River.

A river has a natural constellation. For thousands of years Aborigines had lived there. We now had the chance to care for it, use it and love it. Quite a responsibility.

Had I ever thought about our previous home in quite this way in the past?

Boat imagery took over our everyday life, and Glenn was a natural. Always drawing and planning, and building, beginning with surfboards, then moving on to small sailboats. Glenn was never to lose his excitement in designing and building more advanced Moth sailing boats.

Fun to be had and what fun it was.

For now, back to Bilbao and Frank Gehry.

2014

After Bilbao everything changed for Gehry.

Said to be an interesting architect until Bilbao. After Bilboa he became a transcendental architect who needed to keep on growing, not repeat himself.

He said, "You have to bring your signature to whatever you create. Your language."

"It is important to be yourself, never try to be someone else."

Telling his students. "Be yourself because when you are yourself you are the expert on you, the best

place to be."

From his mother he learnt not to talk down to people, always follow your path.

Be inclusive of others.

Gehry didn't always know exactly what he wanted to do, but he followed his nose. He did whatever, finding ways to be inclusive of others. He knew not everyone would like what he was doing.

"The same number of people who like it will hate it. You do the best you can and let it go."

"Sometimes," he said, "it felt like leaping off a cliff."

Designs were intuitive, not calculated or pre-conceived. The Gehry team often jumped off the cliff together.

Magic for him, and them, is when all the thoughts and ideas in realising the project come together and produce something the world thinks beautiful.

"Lucky when it happens," he said, "Always hoping."

Still today he is curious. He trusts instincts, and is continually poking at things.

He says, "If I knew where I was going all the time, would I always want to go there?"

He likes to let things evolve, maturing like nature.

Creativity surfaced for him on those early days on the floor of his grandmother's kitchen, with tiny blocks of wood. Play for Gehry you imagine is still childlike, questioning, fun, a way of looking for, what?

I doubt he was ever actually sure.

2014

Family for Frank Gehry is the best thing you ever do.

It's complicated but it is worth doing.

If there is a situation where he has to make choices with his time, he chooses Gehry partners and his family.

"I have spent a lot of time worrying and thinking about my kids, struggling with how to help them."

He feels blessed that whatever fame he has been given came when he was in his sixties and seventies.

And now if things do go the other way, up the spout he means, Frank Gehry can gracefully retire.

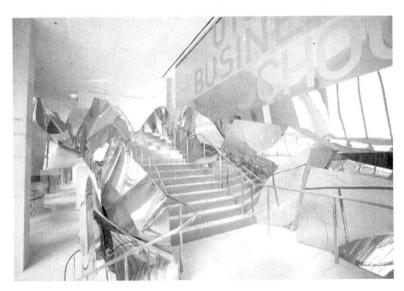

It Begins Right Now

Sometimes it rains
Sometimes I smile

Shards of the poetic
entwined in the lyrical

I fell out of a dream
to live as a part of
our crazy crazy universe.

In My Head I Sit

Beyond negative vibrations inching up the far side of the hill past confusion it will be a lovely day tomorrow eeoow!! remembered days on the river they will always be there in a longing from the slack edges of my skin are we ever who we want to be a patch of light is there in slivers of reflections still to be received what I want today is an aperitif free to write from a rose in the heart & fire in the head a summer of meditation does not make a sparrow thanks for calling eeoow!!! tomorrow is my birthday a yellow-butter-day.

The Land I Came Through

*Weeping decades of
confusion sit on the rim of the bath
unexpected
disquieting not openly discussed
what to say
what to bring together
make whole.*

*Love as catch can loves request
waits close at hand
take note of
the land I once came through.*

It is Right

*not to speak until you need to
speak because you can
not to compromise who you are
speak when you choose to.*

A Tiny Grey Bird

there at my window at the top of the stairs every morning throwing back the covers I crept out of bed stepped to the back of the loft standing very still to watch him dance to hear him sing see him peck at my window he flies away I climbed back into bed thinking wondering and weeks later the first time since forever the tiny grey bird returned to dance and sing his song to me my thoughts spiral bringing to light a song from long ago joy to the world joy to you and to me.

Once

*I heaved myself into a blue lethargy when
the laughter of others could cut me as if
joy was just a hot knife slicing butter.*

*I prized open my closed red doors.
I worked with rocks in The Third Creek
I found life still to be there.*

A Hard Thought

Undone like a plan
beyond skin and history
love like a cloud
speaks the day
skims the tide of afternoon.

Every day is possible
bring me a fortress or
a party about to begin
cease expecting impossible answers
await the off shore breeze
the sum of our parts
drinking in the liquor of lost time
curved wave tells me to soar
past the ephemeral in
tasting sea salt on
the rim of the rock pool.

Some Days Are Diamonds

Self-lacerating honesty forged in a crucible of
loneliness
with honesty there is no place for guilt
in the breeze of tender remorse
mercy close by in ties born of love
belie the anguish
the sweetest music makes pills easier to swallow
take it easy despite the shift
their world is turning right side up
viewed from an incantation of a homeland too long lost
holding the sensitivity to Seven mile beach beneath the bluest of skies
possibilities in the texture of their days holds more than an allusion of
sisters re-awakening, knowing, and accepting one another.

The Missing

*The image of a wild old tree blasted sideways by prevailing winds
leaning into the future shedding days in the autumnal air leaves free
flying dancing viewing the past as a stand-alone fiction threaded with
honey coated nostalgia let go the bitterest of tastes move on ponder
moments of sorrow's resignation indulge in a twitch of immaturity in
haunting sites of youthful things no longer a lock on your heart just
an aching desire feather light to uncork the magic of small things
embedded in your uncontrived days bypassing moments of loss and
regrets home the place where youth once was felt and held no longer
confined to a distant past yet the missing of tinges your life distilling
your existence your grandmother still lives in the curve of joy once
offered you a vivid Madeline moment makes your world a warmer
place without the missing the forgetting could be but a roaring torrent.*

The Architects Tent

Could be a celebrated ballad sitting on a raft set beneath the bluest of skies in a tumble of bleached grass hailed by some as "a remote outback temple" an improbable masterpiece blustery gusts play havoc with his tent home his personal space boiling his kettle on a fire open to the elements he makes a cup of tea constructs a sandwich of goat's cheese and home-grown salad for him at this time there is no better lesson in the architect's language but to hammer a structure of his own making you too are paring back you are not an architect you child-like running jumping leaning into sparseness beyond a clutter of possessions what to hold what to let go you take things out you put things back look for the new in the old no longer held to ransom by loss aware of how little you need to feel joy knowing the exquisite passion in shying away beyond others strange yet sad imaginings to have most simple rewarding conversations with yourself his home not so different from your home stripped bare of the no longer relevant this poem is a story this architect once said "when less is available you will have more time to be who you are the tent maker had once been told by a friend in Sri Lanka that shortly before the Boxing Day tsunami hit she had watched elephants flee for the hills saving her life too by following the elephants feeling things in your bones makes sense to this particular architect.

Words

hang in the mist
embracing
a constant searching appetite.

What Now?

A snake track lean and scribbled in the lee of furred rocks.
A scattering of leaves lay there.
A home looking to the valley.

A coming together.
Waves sweep the shores of Seven Mile Beach.
A sun-filled day.
A speechless end of completion.

What now?
What next?

Rhythms weightless
tugging whimsically
beyond shock waves and
the softly babbling third creek.

Life redefined
between thought and twilight
you letting go of arriving.

Mindfulness

Mindfulness is a mother.
Suffering dwelled in her living.
Take care
love it &
become compliant.

Mindfulness became a mother set free.
Understanding suffering she had a need
to look back to look deeply
to look mindfully.

Shadows born of life cast by stars.
Wisdom a dove released.
I walk on water before climbing out of bed.
I brush my teeth before running to the top of the mountain.
I remember all those everyday heroes.
Touched by warmth
trees smile.

Am I expected to arrive
trumpeting joy?
I know about departures
past thoughts of becoming
past shop- worn attitudes.

I have a never ending capacity
in the hope of being
in the winter I chose to be glad.

Pieces

Maybe I should.
what do I do
when I leave pieces of my life
everywhere I go?

In the butcher shop
in the bank
in the theatre
even in the post office.

I leave them behind
as if they were never mine.
If someone picks them up
what will they do with them?

You Must Stop Asking Why?

Refine yourself
be wise   stop asking questions
fill yourself with
mad skittering nothingness.

Boots

Boots in a box
boots made & bought for walking
in the Himalayas.

Nothing to Do

*for the rest of the afternoon
breakfast is over
the day moves like a yawning snail
teasing a snagged dream.*

*A trembling sky
promises something
tugging at me.
I wonder what the day will demand?*

I hope it loves me.

Pebbles

Pebbles under my feet
soft sand on a beach
rain slips into my mouth
the tip of my tongue dances
on Seven Mile Beach.

Contemplation

The owl in the tree is above me.
My friends I sit here writing to you.
It is cooler here today. I smell the heat of fires burning imagining there
are those who light fires not only for the warmth they offer, but in the
hope of seeing beyond their own catastrophe. Are they burning splint-
tattered wood in a race against themselves & against time, wishing
there would be no tomorrow, needing a way to dance themselves on
and beyond all that is happening to them and around them. After
months of winter I need the sky to open, as a present, my longing so
sweet I can feel the resin of summer sliding out of this wounded tree.
For this owl has sat here listening and sharing my thoughts, caught in
threatening clouds of tension. The owl has perched there above me at
peace with itself and its kingdom in the leafy shadows of our shared
contemplation.

Trust Memory

*Notice the unwashed the unwanted create a way into life's openings
do not crumple dreams will show the way overlapping layers reality
the bridge back the lynch pin in the squeak of stars create what was
not there until you made it yet be there hold close to who you are in
wisps of the yet to be known console and be consoled in the right place
at the right time look beyond yourself trust that there is a significance
to your life too particular to be placed in a box.*

Suspended

In contortion of disorder
slipping through memory like mercury through grass
a continent torn
an island bursting apart
known voices heard a crumbling sound
a strange darkness of light.

A mother gives birth
children saved by calling out
living now in a juggernaut of floating tents
swaying moving rainbow bright
desolation the language of ghosts
waiting
names to be spoken.

A Blue Bowl

fits snugly into
the palm of her hand
the touch of the sun
brings stillness
to soft purple earth.

You Know

Fate declares
time allocates your reality
you blink you let go
you paint a door red
you open it and you walk on and beyond.

Letting Go

Snake tracks cross the feathered earth
I orbit in space

in Chinese crisis represents two characters
danger & hidden opportunity

a brittle sense of normalcy quenches
a once held arc of desolation

in a creek of pebbles
a felled tree sits on a rock

shock waves live in the lee of furred rocks
in a place no longer visited

in shy listening I let go of arriving
renewing my pledge to talk to broken objects

born of the shadows of a long vigil a kite
sails beyond my protective arm of quiet
& the world owes me nothing
I owe the world.

Windows Fall Out of Trees

Promises forget they were made.
In a lived past
trees lose their arms.
Love went missing.
A tightrope walker balanced
in a loneliness so proud
it was intoxicating.

In His Absence

on Seven Mile Beach
wind-scribbled sand dunes
covered in spear grasses.
I stand very still
beside the sea.

A Sheet of Glass

A time comes when you live in an age
of transparency.
You could lose who you are inside yourself
as easily as you could lose yourself in a big city.

All You Do Is

thread your way
into a long
neck- lace of knowing
where the sun shines
between grey and blue
deciding for this moment
to remember
what needs remembering.

Once

Loneliness rose around me
larger than the universe
now flakes of light
sparkle inside me
like phosphorus.

The question is
have I time to be
who I want to be?

A Sweetness Here Tonight

Soon to be on a plane
of to the Himalayas.
A feeling so good my heart aches.

A gaggle of irreverent people
breaking bread and sipping wine with me.
Look at them
the disparate and the desperate
sitting at a table in a restaurant.
I standing on the jetty.
Before a beach barely changed
light fast disappearing.
A yacht slips in from the ocean
drops anchor in the waters
sheltered bay.
City lights flicker in the distance
I'm about to thrust myself   the sharp end of a tool
towards India.

Once Experienced India Never leaves You Alone

Colour chaos and calm.
The Ganges, most holy lets loose the everyday stuff of living.
Your senses compete with sounds constant and loud, horn blowing,
tuk-tuks, buses, rickshaws
motor bikes and bicycles.
A man sleeps on a plot of earth in the middle of a busy road in Calcutta.
A woman drifts by in a colour-filled sari down a mud-filled road in
control of a procession of buffalo.
Centuries distilled into your psyche.
You a stranger fall in love with a people like no other.

Tracks Fall Down the Mountain

against a sky that was

clouds that were

sounds and smells

curl around my chilled ears

ruffling my hair

I write quickly   not wanting to lose words

cold toes

inside my shoes   wiggle

a bird drops

from a tree

to land a breath away.

The Hour is Early in Darjeeling

> Two crisp white pillows
>   at the back of my head   waffled white cotton
> a dog barks
>   air currents   shift   in the wind
> I slip into   yet am divided from
>   I let go thoughts and words
>   close by the sacred mountain
>   Kancthenjunga

On a Silent Mountain

In the Himalayas
I stood before Kanchenjunga
a revered mountain
no longer   do I look for answers.

The Smallest of Ants

have a place to be.
Bees suck sweet juices
from the trumpets of blue delphiniums.
In the garden
on the side of a mountain
at the New Elgin Hotel.
clouds disperse layers of veiled sensuality.
What do I bring   what can I take away of
eye telling stories?

A young man serves breakfast lunch and dinner
his smile lights up the room
cheekily sharing his tricks
a gentle older woman
a black and white chequekered apron
neatly buttoned
a younger woman   jet black hair
eyes of liquid honey   luminous
the light of sunrise.

Untouchable   filled with questions
no language to ask
unspoken words never to be forgotten.

Returning

Flashing lights of a city
whooshing tunnels of traffic
a kaleidoscope
lights flying by.

The taxi-driver talking light and fast
turning his head
scattering words into the back seat &
out through the windows

strands of attention
a calm warmth
filled me the day
I flew home from India.

Wherever I Go, There You Are

1989

In 1989 I wrote a proposal for my final installation at University.

Having read in Chinese, the word CRISIS is represented by two characters.

One DANGER and the other HIDDEN OPPORTUNITIES.

At that time I was still living on the edge of a CRISIS realising I had to let go of any illusions I may have had by opening myself up to the HIDDEN OPPORTUNITIES.

The title "The world owes me nothing, but maybe I owe the world."

Surfacing out of my first journal of reflection at University five years after the yacht Crusader had disappeared in the Bay of Bengal with five young people, the skipper and his little white poodle.

Who loved ice-cream.

A retrospective view of the aftermath of these happenings became the essence of, rather than the actuality of the project, evolving from what was a mixed media installation using writing, and poetry.

I had to find a way to live.

I had no choice.

Becoming a mature-aged University student studying sculpture and textiles was my choice.

2014

Here I am writing of happenings all those years ago.

Beginning in 1977 with a phone call to tell me the yacht Crusader was missing in the Bay of Bengal, after a cyclone had devastated that part of the world. There were yachts that had survived.

This other beginning began in 1985 the year I enrolled at University.

My process of a quest ended with the written word in my final year 1989.

An introspective view, a clearer understanding of what I needed to do, to lead somewhere.

Anywhere.

During and after the completion of four years of creative arts studying Sculpture and textiles my imagination had come alive in ways it never had before, introducing me to my very own fiction.

In 2014 your Thesaurus describes fiction as:

1. An invented idea or statement or narrative, an imaginary thing.
2. Literature esp. novels describing imaginary events and people.
3. Conventionally accepted falsehood. 4. The act or the process
of inventing imaginary things.
Unreal, imaginary, invented, made up, fanciful, mythical, and fictitious.

Had my life before the CHAOS been a fiction of my own making, a life I'd once just fallen into rather than created for myself?
There is a difference between falling into rather than making it mine which I now do more clearly comprehend.
Accepting the soundness of my spirit it's as if my son has offered me an entrée into what was to become, just that, a fiction of my own making.

2014

Glenn would want Fiona and Julie to be an integrated part of what any family, that once was a family, still needs to be.

Together or apart.

Is it an affliction to care too much?

In the past I have struggled with this, often anchoring myself to the heartache of others that wasn't of use to me or anyone. Looking back, caring too much, took up a great part of my life.

Can we ever know what others need?

Is to care an unguarded mutual understanding or just a misnomer? Whatever that is.

Surely to understand is one of the most precious gifts we can offer one another.

Particularly in a family.

The most important thing I must do now is not only to love my children past their times of discontent, without judging their choices. Just love them.

There are things I would have liked to say or do, the doing is often easier than the saying.

I did the best I could. I made my mistakes. I listened. I was just there.

And sometimes listening was like swallowing nails.

There is an age when the choices can only be your children's, good or bad, right or wrong, and then all you can do, support them to the best of your ability.

When things go right for them an unexpected twinge of be-lighted joy can take me by surprise.

To have felt that twinge of joy before I drop off the proverbial twig, and take my final breath could make me very happy.

Longing Rests

Tangled skeins thread themselves through filtered sun
worrying the dust of the day
in a silence not lightly given away
in the liberty of my own compass

Wide white sands run on uninterrupted
heaving waves smooth as glass
unspool on the rim of the ocean
sea-froth toes roam foot- tracked Seven Mile Beach
in the company of experiences beyond
the loss of memory.

Seven Mile Beach

2015

Today I came upon a long lost poem by a Palestinian woman.
Taking me back to those amazing years I once spent working as part of the team at
"Quest for Life" with Petrea King that in some way remains a part of who I became.

This was the poem Petrea once gave me written by the Palestinian Poet. This poem blends with my thinking and the writing of "Where Ever I Go, There You Are." Beginning as a poem and becoming a book.

At Quest for Life people came to sit in what I would call a sacred circle.

When you think you are falling apart, you do what you have to do. I found there was no end
to the reason people come to share time together with Petrea and our team working at Quest.

Some may have lost their bearings, others may have stubbed their toe and didn't know what to
do about it, most were dealing with loss of some kind.

Taking time out for a week at Quest is where goodness, sadness, graciousness and angst in
all its unexpected forms can touch you with the unity and the presence of Petrea holding
harmony at the heart of, what had seemed to be on the first day, a gathering of lost souls.

So much sorrow is not pretty. Life can be ugly.

At the end of our time together you would never have recognized the same circle of people you had met on the first day, diverse though they may have been. Arriving on Monday. Some thinking "What the hell am I doing here."

Kindness

Before you know what kindness really is you must lose things.
Feel the future dissolve in a moment like salt in weakened broth.
What you held in your hand, what you counted and carefully saved, all this must go so you know how desolate the landscape can be between regions of kindness.
How you ride and ride thinking the bus will never stop, the passengers eating maize and chicken will stare out the window forever.
Before you learn the tender gravity of kindness, you must travel where the Indian in a white poncho lies dead by the side of the road. You must see how this could be you, how he too was someone who journeyed through the night with plans and the simple breath that kept him alive. Before you know kindness as the deepest thing inside, you must know sorrow as the other deepest thing. You must wake up with sorrow.
You must speak to it till your voice catches the thread of all sorrow and you see the size of the cloth. Then it is only kindness that makes sense anymore, only kindness that ties your shoelaces and sends you out into the day to mail letters and purchase bread, only kindness that raises its head from the crowd of the world to say it is I you have been looking for, and then goes with you everywhere like a shadow or a friend. By Palestinian poet Naomi Shibab Nye.

2015

I have loved every little bit of Glenn, Fiona, Julie and Kristian from
the day they were born.

Even the annoying bits.

Gob-smacked at what we had created.

Was I a push over, when my love-bucket was filled to overflowing?

I loved being a mother, even those bits I could have done without.

Being sent off to boarding school, so young, was not what I would
have chosen for our three, Glenn, Fiona and Julie.

Yet later having had ten uncles and aunties and their families
to be coddled by.

What a different, loving crazy bunch of a family they all were.

With the grandmother I had, why wouldn't they be?

Giving birth wasn't a walk in the park but it was the most
exciting thing I had ever experienced.

Glenn the first. I could barely wait to repeat my accomplishment.

I felt so clever.

Looking back on life I float-freely in the current of the day, finding
new perspectives even though I am so far down the track. My
thinking today is doing hula hoops.

What I now want is the peacefulness of an ordinary day.

Having brought into fruition a newly planted patch of garden,
a rush of warm summer rain drenches me.

I am left standing in dribbling rain.

Weeping as if my heart could break.

It doesn't.

A no fear factor has forged its way into my lived life.

2015

A long time ago, when Glenn, Fiona and Julie were just little people,
my thinking was . . .

I wanted everything to stay the way it was on that particular day.
Yet changes do happen.
Even at times for the better, in strange yet unexpected ways.
Surprising what can happen.

I hope Glenn would be as proud of us all, as I always was of him.

Today I am alight with an almost gleeful certainty that, If I listen
to myself, and if I hear myself

*I will find the right place to be, with myself and with those I love
and have loved.*

I will listen to my heart.

I open the doors and the windows to air the house and cool the kitchen.
The breeze, earthy, grassed, holds a touch of sunlight.

I Climb the Ladder

Brittle rungs unsteady in the unquiet darkness.
Do not look down.
I check my grip. A cramp hits my leg eeoow!!
Stars whirl I nestle back down under loosening covers.
Night's listening darkness carries stillness.
Soft light imbues my shifting ghost.
In flight from catch calls loosening ties
I balance fate.
Dreams I cannot always pinpoint.
Grant me the solidity of what for me is out there in the ether.
The breeze blows over the mountain tops and through my open windows.
I tug at an imagined ball of string, I wind it up, I scoop the air around me into a torn plastic bag,
gathering in past confusions, disappointments, a myriad of things disguised as clarity.
My body both bereft and amazed.

Stand your ground, be yourself as never before.
Have you ever been unkind?
Possibly?

2015

If Glenn had lived he would be older than you now are, Kristian.

The years have passed. It is as if it were yesterday that Glenn was just a little boy.

You too, Kristian, were once a little boy.

Glenn would have been so happy to have known you.

How happy you too would have been to know him.

What sweet strength there is in just thinking of Glenn?

If Glenn had been standing beside us on the day you, Kristian, had presented me with my first view of the Gehry building. How happy we would all have been.

Pure and undisguised.

Now I just want everyone to be safe.

You, Kristian, Glenn, Fiona and Julie were not always of one mind.

Even within families that is not always the human condition.

Yet I am lighter today.

In 1938 loaded onto a train at Central railway station off to boarding school with a gaggle of people I hadn't even met.

A huge sadness.

All these years later knowing that I have been loved to the point of tears.

I write this with my deepest conviction, Kristian, in the hope that these inconsequential snippets of my lived days that I am sharing with you all could one day be a protection from the hurts or regrets we all carry within us.

Life is for living, Kristian. Truly living with all the rough and tumble of it.

Disappointments just a part of life's flaws is what once jolted me awake to show me things I needed to be aware of. Do we ever cease the need of experiences? Probably not?

I fold back the edges of my days
I climb over thoughts
I hold the rhythms & the oddness of living
in a climate of joy un-cluttered
I step through, & beyond the torn patchwork.

2015

You Kristian, always seemed to have had an unspoken gift, a sense of the preciousness of life from when you were a tiny child.

A gift I once had to dig deep to unearth.

White flowers, they say, are most fragrant at night.

Last week I planted every white flower I could think of.

Roses, alyssum, petunias. Even three different white daisies.

Then completely losing it in buying not just one, but three white hibiscus.

There they were in the plant nursery, spectacularly stepping out from a slow drift of shadows, the white trumpet of each individual flower was quite amazing.

Yet it was just a flower.

Crouching on one knee in the earth a sense of peace had surrounded me.

I had come upon these three white hibiscus. One for Glenn's garden beside the steps curving down from the deck of our home. The other two to be for Fiona, and for Julie.

Glenn's white hibiscus is now nestled in his garden, butted up against the tall, succulent, tumbling plants leading on into the rainforest, scrambling one over the other, vying for space.

It was a strange, but gentle day.

I wish each of them thrive, survive and live well.

2015

Words in a novel have offered me the power to forgive and offer justice.

I turn the last page of Marilynnne Robinson's fruits of a lifetime. Gilead.

Her words tell me that Grace is not so poor a thing, that it cannot reveal itself.

And though I do not share her Christian faith. I am humbled.

Humbled by this simple yet complex book, stunned in the most soothing of ways, taking me to the very heart of the person I would want to be.

There was Gilead sitting on my book-shelf, beside my bed, for years.

Back then it hadn't grabbed me, left on the shelf, untouched, patiently waiting.

Gilead did not have an obtrusive voice.

The day I began to read it, I'd been on a mission, desperate to be taken away from myself. There under a jumble of books was Gilead and I'd begun to read.

I kept on reading, absorbed and compelled by its gentle innate strengths. It's quiet tranquillity.

Simple everyday language, ordinary, yet extra-ordinary writing, her sentences trimmed of ambiguity taking me over, way beyond myself.

Doubts and questions there on every page. Simple doubts, simple questions.

Much of what I do is intuitively instinctual. No real reasoning for what I do or why I do it.

Just seeking for a way to do what now needs to be done.

That is how I find the truth of my experiences. I act on my truth.

I once lived with the illusion that I was the one in charge of my life, and to a degree I was. In the end to find we all have happenings in our lives beyond our control.

The more I accepted this the more I was thankful for the choices I did have.

Have I ever read a happier, or a sadder book?

And do I have a loyalty to my own life in the way Marilynne Robinson has in caring for her characters?

For on their darkest days their light was always there.

A balm to my soul.

Sky- Dream

yourself   into a buzz of

human   interaction   carefully

race against   time   gently

live   joyfully

shape   your day

not   to mention   your heart

2015

The moon is bright tonight.

Darkness could be an intrusion. Testing me.

There have been nights when I was lost to myself.

Not always knowing why.

Then in the early hours of this morning two phone calls arrive, quixotic in the unexpectedness, grown children, Fiona and Julie, each on the same day, offering me homespun homilies.

Different but similar.

What a surprise.

Solemn beauty often works in the schisms and rumblings of living, in attending to the dear ordinary workings of our days.

This is what Gilead has done for me.

This authors three books Gilead, Lila and Home are each about the same two families.

A trilogy

Each book stands alone. And yet together.

Gilead is the first.

Stories about particular members of each of their families.

Both men elderly ministers in a small mid-western town in the 1950's in USA.

A loving, irascible, contrary friendship carried them through their years of living.

Forever entwined.

In their twilight years having spent all of their lives as ministers caring for others, they are now seeking peace in whatever way possible.

Coming closer and closer to the final completion of their lived lives.

2015

It was as if Gilead had touched into feelings in me, both the good and the not so good.

Is there a sacred mystery to sorrow?

Sorrow is but a part of our lives.

There is also great joy.

Gentleness is called for.

Kindness too.

I don't fault myself to have these feelings, doesn't make me a sop or a failure.

I'm not.

I run my own race. I live in my own thinking.

I make my own choices.

Not in eccentricity.

Maybe a little capricious whimsy.

Best others try not to understand what I write about.

Often not sure myself.

I paid attention to the breeze. It changed all day.

Floating.

A presence I haven't thought too much about.

The way I don't think about very religious people, who it seems to me are so often taken away from their own precious thinking by their strict adherences to man-made religious practices.

Some religious thinkers do have the potency of the self-righteous, holier than thou thinking.

What would I know?

Marilynne Robinson's Gilead maybe knows and writes much about religious life in a different, more subtle, way.

Her stories take in the whole of life's simple yet chaotic happenings.

2015

The way our treatment of the first people of this land, the aborigines, indicates to me a complete lack of so, called religious caring.

As in Gilead you find the color of your skin in 1950's America could at times have been the cause of a great deal of heartache for many.

In a country appearing to be quite religious.

People can change. Everything can change, the way I watched changes happen when my Aboriginal students found their way into their creativity that had been so exciting to be a part of for seven years.

Silkscreening students and class teacher,
Faye McDonald.

2015

Meditation has not softened my thinking of late.

Yet reading Gilead seems to have softened many things.

As I said, words are poor things. Words are what I have. And they have served me well.

Why is it that the solemn reasoning of Marilynne Robinson's words in Gilead have me today teetering on these huge moss-covered boulders before crossing to the other side of "The Third Creek"?

My self-proclaimed creek?

A puff of wind and a drift of mist slips beyond the rainforest, wafting down towards the valley.

A long- tailed magpie takes alarm.

The cicadas suddenly silent.

I jump from boulder to boulder over the gurgling rush of water not far from the home I built and have lived in for a long time.

What richness!!!

This is the creek I once worked in, creating cairns to memory, rock by rock, day by day in the early hours. The richness once offered to me, the space to share another's land to create a new beginning.

Now Marilynne's Gilead is offering me something very different.

I have I in the past been a sceptic of man-made religion?

Maybe my reading of Gilead is the way others read their bibles?

An enlightening, exquisitely measured portrait of families, together or apart.

Here are we each living in a self-proclaimed heart-sick world gone haywire?

Wafting our way through chance moments hour by hour.

Voices catching us unaware come to us from all over the world. Here I stand in the creek on a moon-white day leaning into myself. The trees remember me, standing here on a boulder in "The Third Creek."

Unmotivated Joy fills me with a corny delight.

An echo of a didgeridoo. Sounds soft and slow.

A child laughs.

A sailboat bumps the jetty.

Quivering, I lift my face to the heavens. I breathe in light, to a connection beyond time.

Beneath shadowy clouds, waves wash in and out onto the white sandy shores of Seven Mile Beach.

2015

No life was entirely crushed by misapprehensions.

Fiction uncovers the delight to be found in a folk ballad about ordinary lives.

Breaking open, a cartload of characters not standing up for themselves, afraid to show who they are, wishing they could have their time again. But they can't.

Neither can I.

Too late to square the plate if it needs squaring.

Shrink not from mishaps, taut images, seeing further than you ever have before, your days not unlike the slow winding down of a clock, the pulse of a fertile life, adapting, shifting.

A loose concept.

Live in lanes still to be travelled.

Step beyond things that once would once have gobbled you up.

But they didn't.

Not yet.

My Grandmother

soaks the sand at my feet
steeping in as blood and memory
my touch stone.

Once a living evocative cultural traveller
a sense of delicacy shimmering in a rare fragility
returning me to her country.
Unframed she lived, unbounded by pigments inks and water colors
her language quite beautiful
associations and belongings
all things for my grandmother were possible.

127

2015

Lost white sails, the white belly of a dove, the place you face alone.
Crisis propels us forward beyond ourselves.
The truth of this is surprising.
Useless to struggle, taste the rush of life crystallising, gaps and silences.
Luminosity and forgetting.
In the light of suspension our hearts see beyond assumptions.
A break in life's patterns, beyond the thin threads of what could have been. No relief in blaming others, no matter how difficult things may have been.
Masks fall away when there truly is a crisis.
Smiling and weeping at fates not so simple reversals beyond the edge of failures.
There have been times when I couldn't write.
I could not read.
I felt beyond feeling.
Through tangled skeins my skin captures the value of silence in the liberty of my own company.
I walk on uninterrupted.
Waves smooth as glass unspool on the edge of the ocean.
Sea froth slips through my toes, beach tracks pass beyond my lens of memory.

Am I afraid of my imagination?
Do some find imagination scary and eternally soporific?
Uninspiring?
Strong on starts, loose on endings, less certain of exploration, tension taut, dialogue sharp, sitting on the edge of living.
My interior life is becoming stronger and sweeter.
It fills the empty spaces, pares me back, leading me toward my place of refuge.
My interior space.

2015

I once wrote my life in stones, tuned to the earth in the fast running "Third Creek".

The longer I worked in the creek the more I was transformed in a landscape deeply still.

And I remember.

Once talking to myself in "The Third Creek" as if I were not alone.

Yet I was.

Others may have thought me crazy.

But I wasn't.

This poem was always there with me. This poem is with me still.

I hold the poem the way I will want always to hold the gaze of Glenn, Fiona, Julie and Kristian.

Wanting to hold them without holding them.

Wanting to be with them without being with them.

Breathless heart in mouth.

Looking for, in his honour, what we could each become.

For in our homes, truth was always told in the kitchen.

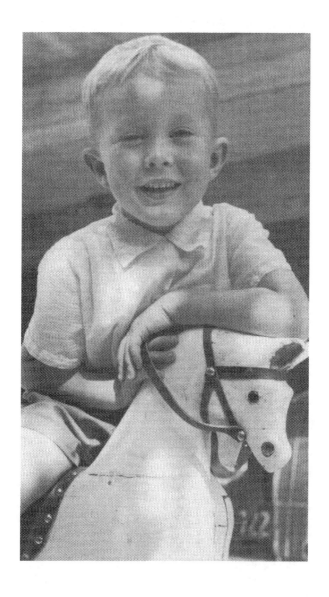

The Present

Quiet straight an island's surface carries water's language
less calculated than tides
the twist of autumn lets down the light of winters spoken form and
force
high above pre-empted words soar into nights fast abiding sense of
    whispered beauty
detailed space surrendered
wind falls under the sun
light leans in from the left
breathes the sweat of dreams
wounded curled up hurtles along a road no longer there
skirts a past now less thought of than soup tins clothes pegs or
    biscuits feathered in the fall of snow
in the early hours slivers of the yet to be spins you aloft
seek life in the slant of morning broken open just around the corner
to reveal the ambient pathways of your sleeping Ghost.

fay marie mcdonald

My heartfelt thanks to all the writers I have ever read throughout my long life.

This book began as a poem, eventually becoming "Where Ever I Go, There You Are"

Barbara Isenberg's book Conversations with Frank Gehry was important. A gift from Kristian.

The Brooke Davis book "Lost and Found" and her article "Relearning the world"

Marilynne Robinsons heartfelt book Gideon.

My family Glenn, Fiona, Julie and Kristian for just being my children. And Caroline.

Beth and her family for the continuing friendship of being offered a space to be.

John my partner for his support in so many ways. And his children.

My choice in words and pictures trailing through the meanderings of, the memories of, in moving towards the sharing of, my experiences and thoughts of a lived life.

Meanderings that may not be important to my family yet are important to me.

Of my fantastic much younger writing partners, "The Thursday Group," for so many years.

Linda, Sue, Ali, Elizabeth and Andrea.

To Mandy whose beautiful painting is once again the cover for the second book that is the companion to Grief is a River.

The title of this book is Where Ever I Go, There You Are.

To Jason for his untiring help to connect and arrange words, photographs and his sensitive support in guiding and giving me the help I needed to bring my book to completion.

I could not have achieved the completion of this book without the combination of both John and Jason.

Finally I wish Joy to the world. To all the little fishes in the deep blue sea, and most of all I wish joy to you. And to me.